I AM A CREATIVE, SPEAKING SPIRIT

Volume 2 of the *I Know Who I Am* Series

I0163085

By Lenita Reeves

Other titles from Lenita Reeves

I Am Predestined

I Am: The Divine Purpose Manifesto

Watchman Responsibility: Winning the End-Time Warfare to Stand Watch and Pray Effectively

How to Teach the Bible with Excellence: Answering the Call to the Teaching Ministry

Fervent Fire: Understanding the Pattern of the Priesthood for Prevailing Intercessory Prayer

The Spirit of Rejection: Heal its Wounds, Restore your Self-Esteem, and Move on to Promotion

Breaking the Silence: The Journey from Rape to Redemption

All available at major online retailers!

Book Description

I Am a Creative, Speaking Spirit
Volume 2 of the *I Know Who I Am* Series

The *I Know Who I Am* series focuses on your identity in Christ and the wonderful, yet often misunderstood, realities of being created in the image and likeness of God. Each volume is a building block for the construction of rightly-focused self-confidence, which is necessary to win in life and take dominion.

If you are unsure of what life holds or tempted to look down on yourself, feel inadequate, or succumb to negative self-talk, this series will give insight to the reality of who you are, and lift your confidence to where it belongs.

Volume 2, I Am a Creative, Speaking Spirit, begins by examining the image of God in which you were created and the difference between soul and spirit. When God created the heavens and the earth, He spoke them into existence. That same creative power is in you. In this volume, you discover the power that lies within you and the unlimited nature of the realm from which you came. Get ready to be lifted and boldly declare, "I know who I am."

From the Series

I Know Who I Am:
Truths You Need for Confident, Purposeful Living

I AM A CREATIVE, SPEAKING SPIRIT

By Lenita Reeves

PurposeHouse Publishing
Copyright © 2018

*P*urpose*H*ouse
Publishing

Lenita Reeves is the founder of the APT Apostolic and Prophetic Network and of *Breaking the Silence: The Journey from Rape to Redemption* and more. For more information, visit www.lenitareeves.org.

PurposeHouse Publishing, Columbia, Maryland.

ISBN-13: 978-0-9963647-5-1

Cover design by PurposeHouse Publishing.

Unless otherwise indicated, all scriptural quotations are from the King James Version (KJV) of the Bible.

Scripture from New King James Version, Copyright © 1982 by Thomas Nelson, Inc. All rights reserved.

Scripture from Amplified Bible, Copyright © 1987 by the Lockman Foundation. (www.Lockman.org)

Scripture from the Message Bible, Copyright © 1993, 1994, 1995, 1996, 2000, 2001, 2002 by Eugene H. Peterson. All rights reserved.

Scripture from the New International Version, Copyright © 1973, 1978, 1984 by Biblica.

Scripture from the New Living Translation, Copyright © 1996, 2004 by Tyndale Charitable Trust.

Dedication

For the body of Christ, the priesthood of believers, that sometimes forgets its own greatness.

Epigraph

I know who I am. – Author

Acknowledgments

I am grateful for the example of our Lord, Jesus. Even though his own brothers did not believe in him, he continued to believe and publicly declare, "I am." (John 7:5)

I AM A CREATIVE, SPEAKING SPIRIT

By Lenita Reeves

From the *I Know Who I Am* Series

Introduction

Have you ever met someone and secretly admired their confidence? Some people exude confidence—not in a loud or obnoxious way. They are simply firm in their convictions, comfortable in their own skin, and at peace with their strengths and weaknesses. If anyone should exude this quiet strength, shouldn't God's children?

Yet most don't know who God says they are or the promises at their disposal. They know only that they are saved from hell, that if they die today, they will go to heaven because they have believed and confessed Jesus as Lord. Sadly, they still carry all kinds of issues that affect their confidence for victorious daily living and question the purpose of their lives. Worse still, some are not even convinced of their salvation, and even more do not walk with a resonating reality of who God has made them, where they stand with God, and where they are in their destinies.

The pages of this book have the power to eliminate low living, transform timid mindsets into bold ones, and release greatness hidden underneath the masks of doubt and unbelief. If you are ready for a new reality—a new self-concept—grounded in the truth of the Word, don't stop reading until you've finished the entire series.

It's time for the revelation of kingdom realities that will transform the way you see yourself and how you live your daily life. Get ready to leave your old mindset(s) behind!

Volume 2: I Am a Creative, Speaking Spirit

Something went wrong. Darkness and confusion took over. Not even a pinhead of light could be found. God called a meeting in heaven. He sat on His throne and began to take counsel with His Son. Things weren't looking good. The cherubs could tell there was something at hand, but they couldn't fully understand the discussion around the throne.

Look, I've spent the last five days creating all these things, but there's nothing here that reflects our glory—our likeness. Let's make an agent on earth that reflects our image and likeness to have dominion over everything I have spoken into existence these past five days. "Let us make man in our image and after our likeness," He said (Genesis 1:26).

The godhead was in agreement. So, He proceeded. God created man in his own image, in the image of God created He him; male and female created He them (Genesis 1:27).

This was the beginning of the sixth day of creation. On that day, God not only creatively spoke into existence the thing called man but also formed man's fleshly earth suit from the dust of the ground and breathed into him *pneuma*—wind—spirit. This is the only day of creation that we see God breathing into what He created because this is the only day during which male and female—humankind—was created.

In that day lies the reality that you are not just flesh—you are made in the image and likeness of God. "What is that image and likeness?" you ask. Put simply, the answer is *spirit*.

> "...***God is Spirit***, and those who worship Him must worship in spirit and truth." (John 4:24, New King James Version, emphasis added)

Because we live in this world that bombards us with its messages, cares, and concerns, the reality that we are spirit beings is drowned out and eludes us. But God said, "Let us make man in our image and likeness," and God himself is *spirit*. He spoke creation into existence and that exact likeness is inside of you—the ability to speak things into existence. You are not a human being—you are a speaking, spirit being.

> ... even God, who quickeneth the dead, and calleth those things which be not as though they were. (Romans 4:17b, King James Version)

> Death and life are in the power of the tongue: and they that love it shall eat the fruit thereof. (Proverbs 18:21, King James Version)

Again, you are not a human being! You should not confess, "I'm only human." God's DNA, which is spirit-DNA, is in you. According to the Word of God, there is a spirit in you, and it's the *real* you:

> But there is a spirit in man, And the breath of the Almighty gives him understanding. (Job 32:8, New King James)

THERE IS A SPIRIT IN YOU, AND IT'S THE REAL YOU!

Years ago, I had an experience that convinced me of this truth. I attended one of Wellington Boone's New Generation Ministries (NGM) Leadership Training Schools. It was basically a boot camp for Christian campus ministry leaders. We had to be ready for physical training at 5am, carrying wooden crosses inscribed with our identification numbers on our backs, and every time we exercised, we carried those crosses the entire time to grow our appreciation of the pain Jesus endured walking to Golgotha and hanging on the cross.

Morning prayer, which always lasted more than an hour, followed physical training. After that, we all really needed showers! We were also required to fast until the afternoon.

One day, we went straight from morning prayer into a teaching session with one of the many anointed pastors they brought in to train us. It happened to be Bishop Larry Jackson (then Pastor Jackson) of Bethel Outreach International Church in Charlotte, North Carolina. Using the example of Moses, he began teaching about leadership. Then, something he said really hit me. I don't know if it was because my body was so tired that I didn't realize it until after it happened, but in reaction to what he said, my spirit spoke out, Hallelujah! It was loud, and it wasn't my mind speaking. It came from some other place inside me. You know, one of those moments that the religious folks in the church get annoyed by, even though it doesn't bother God because someone is being blessed? Before I could realize what had come out of me, the whole group turned to look at me. In hindsight, there had to be something different for them to all turn and look at me. They had to have recognized that there was something different about it as well.

It took a second for my mind to come back to me, but with everyone looking at me, I realized that my spirit had spoken out and my conscious mind (soul) had not been involved. My body was so tired from the physical training, fasting, and praying in the spirit beforehand that I'm not even sure my lips moved—really. I mean it. It undoubtedly, unequivocally came out of my spirit. My mind had not been involved.

You see, it was an answer to prayer. After reading Hebrews 4:12 one day during the Leadership Training School, I had been praying and asking God to help me understand the difference between the spirit and soul. According to Hebrews 4:12, the Word of God is quick and sharper than any two-edged sword and it can separate the soul from the spirit.

ONE OF THE THINGS THE WORD OF GOD IS ABLE TO DO IS SEPARATE THE SOUL FROM THE SPIRIT.

I had thought to myself, "How could my spirit be separated from my soul? If that's possible, they must be two different things."

> For the word of God is quick, and powerful, and sharper than any two-edged sword, piercing even to the ***dividing asunder of soul and spirit***, and of the joints and marrow, and is a discerner of the thoughts and intents of the heart (Hebrews 4:12 King James Version, emphasis added)

For the Word that God speaks is alive and full of power [making it active, operative, energizing, and effective]; it is sharper than any two-edged sword, penetrating to ***the dividing line of the breath of life (soul) and [the immortal] spirit***, and of joints and marrow [of the deepest parts of our nature], exposing and sifting and analyzing and judging the very thoughts and purposes of the heart. (Hebrews 4:12 Amplified Bible Classic Edition, emphasis added)

Well, I got my answer! At that moment in class, and with everyone looking at me, I knew without a doubt that the soul is limited to rationale and reasoning. The spirit supersedes rationale and reasoning. Spirit calls unto spirit. That is why it pays to obey God even when it doesn't make sense. My spirit had connected with the Word of God that Pastor Jackson was teaching—in a real way. It was a *rhema, a spoken word of divine revelation,* that had watered my spirit. And I will never forget that moment.

THE SPIRIT SUPERSEDES RATIONALE AND REASONING. THAT'S WHY IT PAYS TO OBEY GOD

EVEN WHEN IT DOESN'T MAKE SENSE.

Please believe that the real you is a speaking spirit. Inside of your body (your flesh) is the real you—your spirit. For to be absent from the body is to be present with the Lord. If your body is dead (absent), what is *the you* that is present with the Lord? It is your spirit!

> For as the body without the spirit is dead, so faith without works is dead also. (James 2:26, King James Version)

It was the *pnuema, the wind of His very own Spirit*, which God breathed into man that quickened man's soul and body. Without the spirit, the brain ceases (reasoning capacities cease). Without the breath of the spirit, the soul and the body cease to function.

THE BODY WITHOUT THE SPIRIT IS DEAD!

> And the Lord God formed man of the dust of the ground, and breathed into his nostrils the breath of life; and

man became a living being. (Genesis
2:7, New King James Version)

I know that we are used to hearing that
man became a living soul and, thus, think
of ourselves as rational beings—souls; but
consider that many translations do not use
the word soul. Look at these translations:

Then the Lord God formed the man
from the dust of the ground. He
breathed the breath of life into the
man's nostrils, and the man became a
living person. (Genesis 2:7, New
Living Translation, italics added)

Then the Lord God formed a man
from the dust of the ground and
breathed into his nostrils the breath
of life, and the man became a living
being. (Genesis 2:7, New
International Version)

Then the Lord God formed [that is,
created the body of] man from the
dust of the ground, and breathed into
his nostrils the breath of life; and the
man became a living being [an
individual complete in body and

spirit]. (Genesis 2:7, Amplified Bible)

Then the Lord God formed man of dust from the ground, and breathed into his nostrils the breath of life; and man became a living being. (Genesis 2:7, New American Standard Bible)

There is no life without the spirit! Actually, the word translated soul in the King James Version is *nephesh*, which means "breathing creature." In other words, there was no life in that dust of the ground we call Adam until God breathed His Spirit into it. That continuous process of breathing that you and I take for granted every day didn't take place in Adam until God first breathed into him His own Spirit, and human beings have been breathing ever since. Glory to God! He's awesome. No doctor could have done that.

THAT CONTINUOUS PROCESS OF BREATHING THAT YOU AND I TAKE FOR GRANTED EVERYDAY DIDN'T TAKE PLACE IN ADAM UNTIL GOD FIRST BREATHED INTO HIM HIS OWN SPIRIT. A SINGLE BREATH STILL PERSISTS THROUGH ALL

HUMANITY—THE BREATH OF GOD.

The real you is not body or soul. The real you that gives life to everything else about you is spirit! God created Adam before he formed him of the dust of the ground. What God created was Adam's spirit. He then formed his earth suit, his body.

So you *are* a spirit, you possess a soul, and you live in an earth suit called a body. 1 Thessalonians 5:23 supports this:

> And the very God of peace sanctify you wholly; and I pray God your whole *spirit and soul and body* be preserved blameless unto the coming of our Lord Jesus Christ. (1 Thessalonians 5:23 KJV, italics added)

Too many believers don't understand the power that rests in the truth that they are spirit beings. They quote the scripture, "The spirit is willing, but the flesh is weak." Yes, there may be times when you will stumble in the flesh. If you say you are without sin, the truth is not in you. And it is helpful to understand that your flesh is not the real you, so you don't get stuck in condemnation when you yield to it. It is your spirit that is regenerated when you are born again.

> Not by works of righteousness which we have done, but according to his mercy he saved us, by the washing of regeneration, and renewing of the Holy Ghost. (Titus 3:5 King James Version)

Your flesh doesn't get born again because it's not of the divine nature that God breathed into you. It is merely a necessity for functioning in this earthly environment—an earth suit.

You have been given tools to build up your spirit, so it won't remain at a disadvantage to your flesh. Paul, who in Romans 7 talked about the war between the flesh and the spirit, gave us the key in 1 Corinthians 9:27 when he said, "I discipline my body and bring it under subjection so that after having preached to others, I myself might not be a castaway." Consider these two versions of this scripture.

> I discipline my body like an athlete,

training it to do what it should. Otherwise, I fear that after preaching to others I myself might be disqualified. (1 Corinthians 9:27, New Living Translation)

But I discipline my body and make it my slave, so that, after I have preached to others, I myself will not be disqualified. (1 Corinthians 9:27, New American Standard Bible)

Is your body your spirit's slave? That's the way it's supposed to be. Your body is supposed to be a vehicle your spirit drives in order to complete your purpose journey. The more your flesh is under subjection to your spirit, the greater works you will do and the higher dimension of purpose you live.

YOUR BODY IS SUPPOSED TO BE A VEHICLE YOUR SPIRIT DRIVES IN ORDER TO COMPLETE YOUR PURPOSE JOURNEY.

Your spirit is what gives life to everything else about you, so please discipline your flesh and prioritize your spirit! Focus on the things of the Spirit. Stop thinking that you are only human and, therefore, can never overcome certain sins. Don't allow human reasoning to negate the strength of your spirit.

The stronger your flesh, the weaker your spirit will be. The stronger your reasoning against obedience, the weaker your spirit will be. Arm your spirit with the *Sword of the Spirit*, which, according to Galatians 6:17, is the Word of God. Obey Jude 20 and spend time building up your spirit by praying in the Holy Ghost. Consistently take steps to prioritize your spirit, and you will find that you will grow not only faster but also in a healthier manner than other believers. Keep the fire of prayer burning. Don't let your candle grow dim.

> The spirit of man is the candle of the Lord, searching all the inward parts of the belly. (Proverbs 20:27, King James Version)

You are more than what people see with their physical eyes! You are a speaking spirit!

OTHER TITLES

- *I Am: The Divine Purpose Manifesto*
- *I Am a Creative, Speaking Spirit*
- *Watchman Responsibility: Winning the End-Time Warfare to Stand Watch and Pray Effectively*
- *How to Teach the Bible with Excellence: Answering the Call to the Teaching Ministry*
- *Fervent Fire: Understanding the Pattern of the Priesthood for Prevailing Intercessory Prayer*
- *The Spirit of Rejection: Heal its Wounds, Restore your Self-Esteem, and Move on to Promotion*
- *Breaking the Silence: The Journey from Rape to Redemption*
- *Understanding the Power of Agreement: A Necessary Key for Prayer, Relationships, and Progress*
- *Pentecost and the Promise of the Spirit: Understanding the New Covenant, Holy Spirit, and His Gifts*

Now Available from
PurposeHouse Publishing

An Anchor for My Soul:
Soul Stabilizing Devotions for the
Multifaceted, Multi-tasked Woman
by Lenita Reeves

Have you ever asked, "Why do I have to do everything myself?" Today's Christian woman is faced with a dilemma, and its name is "multi." While striving to serve the Lord, multiplicities of responsibility vie for her attention. She wrestles to handle it all and, at the same time, come to grips with her own multifaceted nature. The duty of serving others often overtakes her need for peaceful, quiet times of individual refueling.

An Anchor for My Soul addresses this issue, facilitates "me time," and anchors Christian women who are dizzy and discombobulated from the potter's wheel. Before a ship sets sail, it must be anchored and refueled. This 21-day devotional is the multi-tasked, multifaceted woman's necessary daily dose of anchoring and refueling.

Connect with Dr. Lenita!

Discover the latest tools and encouragement for living on purpose! Visit (or click) https://www.lenitareeves.org/ and join our mailing list for the latest blog posts and continued news and previews of other upcoming books.

Visit us on social media

Web:
www.lenitareeves.org

Facebook:
http://www.facebook.com/pastorlenita

Instagram:
http://www.instagram.com/pastorlenita

About the Author
Dr. Lenita Reeves

Everyone has fallen but some are in need of the inspiration required to get back up. Through fresh insight delivered in an approachable manner with a twist of real-life humor, Lenita Reeves inspires audiences to get back up. She is the Founder of PurposeHouse Christian Counseling and the APT Apostolic and Prophetic Network. Some call her preacher, and some call her teacher, but all agree that she is a prolific voice who speaks with transparency, highlighting her highs as well as her lows to show others that God can turn pain into a platform and use the foolish things of this world to confound the wise.

As a rape survivor and former teen mom, God has graced Lenita to be an outspoken overcomer, sharing her testimony freely and as a result, seeing captives set free all over the world. She is an international speaker and member of the RAINN speaker's bureau. She has traveled as a featured conference speaker in the US, London, Jamaica, Haiti, the Bahamas, Kenya, Uganda, and Ghana, and is the author of several books, all available at http://www.lenitareeves.org/books-by-lenita. From senior class president to founder of a non-profit, leadership has been an evident mark of Lenita's calling and passions. She has a Bachelor of Science in Industrial Engineering, a Master of Arts in Dance Education, an MBA, and a doctorate in Christian Counseling. She attended Beulah Heights Bible College in Atlanta, Georgia.

A unique blend of education, experiences, and talents positions Lenita to address topics such as: women in leadership, personal leadership discovery, healing from abuse, understanding the purpose of the marriage bed and more. From the brokenhearted to businesspersons to board members, Lenita can relate articulately to their unique challenges.

If you are ready to be inspired by a speaker, if your audience needs to get back up, or just needs a jolt of fresh energy to go to the next level, contact Lenita today. For more information, visit www.lenitareeves.org.

www.ingramcontent.com/pod-product-compliance
Lightning Source LLC
Chambersburg PA
CBHW060102050426
42448CB00011B/2580